Power Rangers™ Combat Evil Puzzles and Mazes

Cover Design by TXF Graphics
Illustrated by Dwayne Ferguson
Cheryl Saban, Senior Editor

TM and © 1994 Saban Entertainment, Inc. & Saban International N.V. All Rights Reserved. MIGHTY MORPHIN POWER RANGERS and all logos, character names and distinctive likenesses thereof are trademarks of Saban Entertainment, Inc., and Saban International N.V.

Copyright © 1994 Modern Publishing, a division of Unisystems, Inc. ® Honey Bear Books is a trademark owned by Honey Bear Productions, Inc., and is registered in the U.S. Patent and Trademark Office.

No part of this book may be reproduced or copied without written permission from the publisher. All Rights Reserved.

Modern Publishing
A Division of Unisystems, Inc.
New York, New York 10022
Printed in the U.S.A.

W9-CGK-350

1.

Who are the Mighty Morphin Power Rangers? To find out, follow the correct letter path to spell a message that describes them.

SEE ANSWERS.

Use the chart below to decode a message from the
Power Rangers.

A	B	C	D	E	F	G	H	I	J	K	L	M
1	2	3	4	5	6	7	8	9	10	11	12	13

N	O	P	Q	R	S	T	U	V	W	X	Y	Z
14	15	16	17	18	19	20	21	22	23	24	25	26

‾‾ ‾ ‾‾ ‾   ‾‾ ‾ ‾‾ ‾‾ ‾‾ ‾‾ ‾   ‾ ‾‾   ‾ ‾‾
18 9 20 1   18 5 16 21 12 19 1   9 19   1 14

‾ ‾‾ ‾ ‾‾   ‾‾ ‾‾ ‾‾ ‾ ‾ ‾‾ ‾ ‾‾ ‾‾.
5 22 9 12   19 15 18 3 5 18 5 19 19

SEE ANSWERS.

3.
Follow the path from Zordon to the teens so that he can give them the Power Morphers.

START.

FINISH.

SEE ANSWERS

Cross out the letters with a ⚡. Then write the remaining letters in the order in which they appear to read the message.

⚡	♦	⚡	#	♦	♦	⚡	*	♦	♦
R	T	U	H	E	D	L	I	N	O
♦	⚡	♦	*	⚡	♦	♦	⚡	⚡	#
Z	G	O	R	M	D	S	V	Q	C
♦	♦	*	♦	⚡	#	♦	♦	⚡	⚡
H	A	N	G	P	E	I	N	T	Y
*	♦	⚡	♦	♦	⚡	⚡	*	⚡	#
T	O	Q	M	E	L	A	G	O	A
⚡	⚡	⚡	♦	⚡	♦	⚡	*	♦	⚡
P	J	N	Z	A	O	B	R	D	C

___ _____

_____ ____

_____!

SEE ANSWERS.

5.
Follow the path that takes the Yellow Ranger from one end of the Sabertooth Tiger Dinozord to the other.

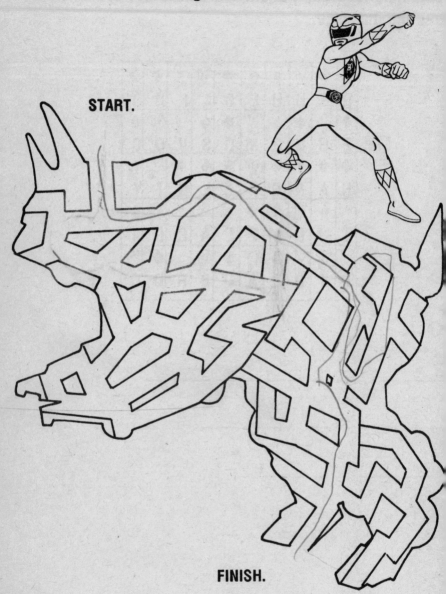

START.

FINISH.

SEE ANSWERS.

6.

Follow the correct path to spell the name of the Power Ranger who drives the Mastodon Dinozord.

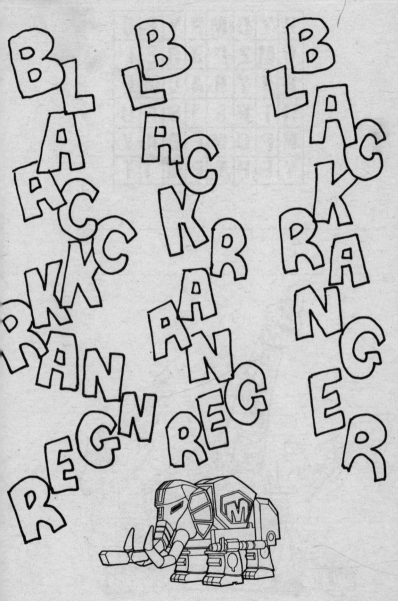

SEE ANSWERS.

Cross out every letter that appears 5 times. Then write the remaining letters backwards to read the message.

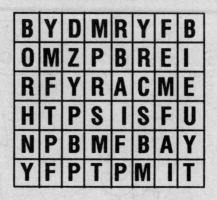

B	Y	D	M	R	Y	F	B
O	M	Z	P	B	R	E	I
R	F	Y	R	A	C	M	E
H	T	P	S	I	S	F	U
N	P	B	M	F	B	A	Y
Y	F	P	T	P	M	I	T

_ _ _ _ _ _ _ _   _ _   _ _ _

_ _ _ _ _ _ _ _   _ _ _ _ .

SEE ANSWERS.

ill in the missing vowels (AEIOU) to spell the names of
he teens who become Power Rangers.

1. T R _ N _
2. B _ L L Y
3. Z _ C K
4. K _ M B _ R L Y
5. J _ S _ N

SEE ANSWERS.

9.

Help the Blue Ranger break free from the clutches of Baboo. Which path leads him to safety?

START.

FINISH.

SEE ANSWERS

0.

Unscramble the letters to spell the name of a Dinozord that resembles an elephant.

TAONODMS

_ _ _ _ _ _ _ _

SEE ANSWERS.

11.
Draw your own King Sphinx.

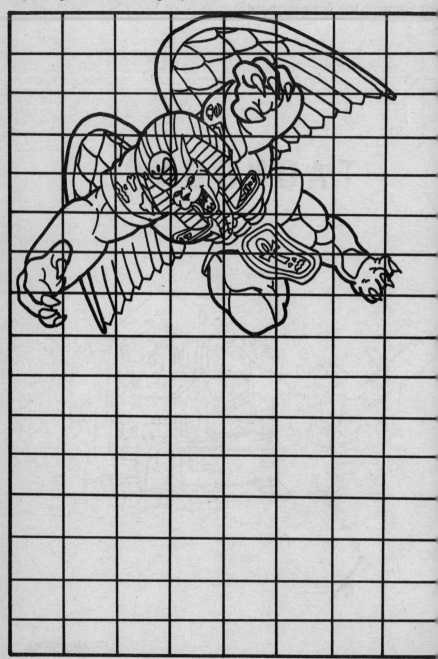

SEE ANSWERS

2.

Rita Repulsa's Evil Space Aliens are a motley crew of criminals. Lead the Power Rangers to their hiding place.

START.

FINISH.

SEE ANSWERS.

13.

Drop a letter in column A to spell a new word in column B. (You can rearrange the letters to spell the new word.) Then write the dropped letter in the circle to spell the mystery word.

A	B	
ZEST		◯
OPEN		◯
RATE		◯
CARD		◯
MOAT		◯
ANT		◯

SEE ANSWERS

4.

he Red Ranger has summoned the Tyrannosaurus inozord. Which path unites them?

START.

FINISH.

SEE ANSWERS.

15.

Drop a letter in column A to spell a new word in column B. (You can rearrange the letters to spell the new word.) Then write the dropped letter in the circle to spell the mystery name.

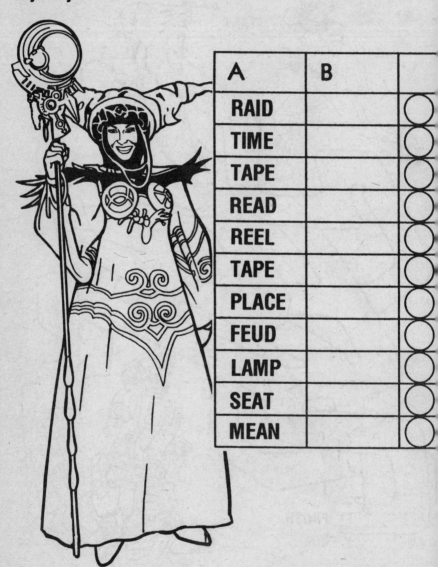

A	B	
RAID		○
TIME		○
TAPE		○
READ		○
REEL		○
TAPE		○
PLACE		○
FEUD		○
LAMP		○
SEAT		○
MEAN		○

SEE ANSWERS.

Alpha 5 leads the teens to the Command Center and to a meeting with Zordon. Which trail does he take?

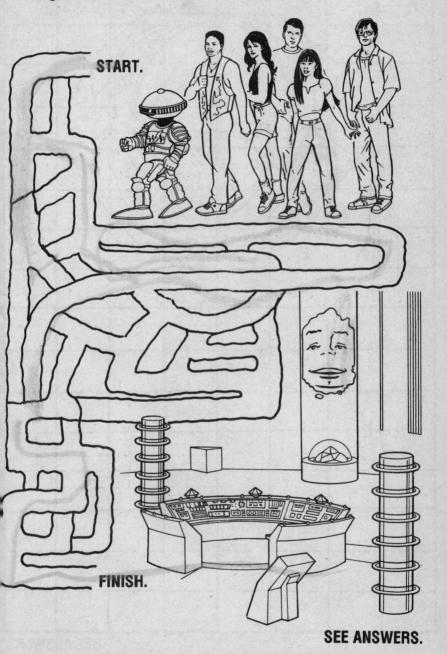

START.

FINISH.

SEE ANSWERS.

17.
Draw your own Power Morpher.

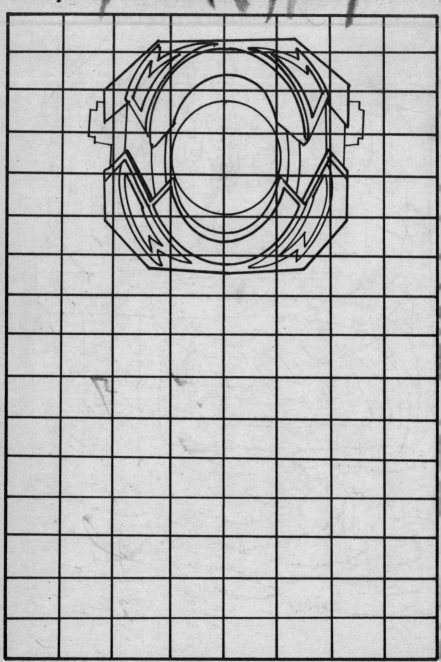

SEE ANSWERS.

8.

The Putty Patrol retreats. Which path does it take to flee?

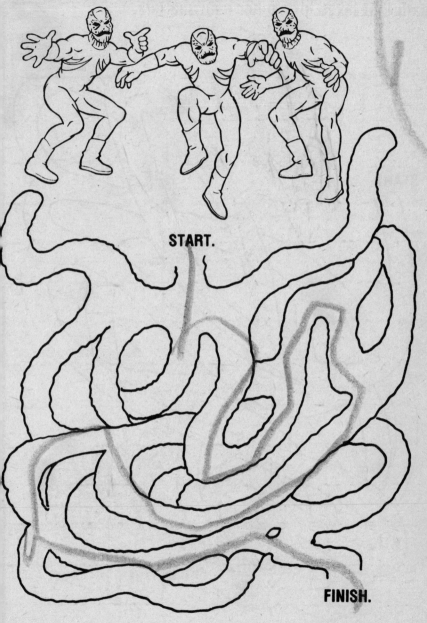

START.

FINISH.

SEE ANSWERS.

19.
Squatt must deliver a message to Rita Repulsa. Pick the path that takes him to her headquarters.

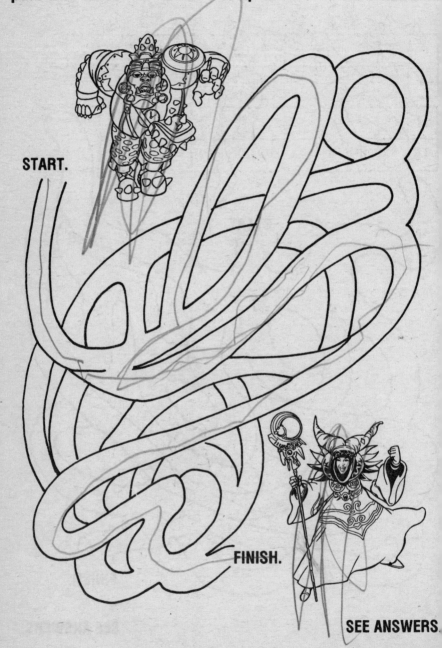

START.

FINISH.

SEE ANSWERS.

20.

Use the chart below to decode a message from the
Power Rangers.

A	B	C	D	E	F	G	H	I	J	K	L	M
1	2	3	4	5	6	7	8	9	10	11	12	13

N	O	P	Q	R	S	T	U	V	W	X	Y	Z
14	15	16	17	18	19	20	21	22	23	24	25	26

__ __ __   __ __ __ __ __   __ __ __ __ __ __ __
20 8 5   16 15 23 5 18   18 1 14 7 5 18 19

__ __ __   __ __ __ __ __ __ '__
1 18 5   5 1 18 20 8 19

__ __ __ __   __ __ __ __!
15 14 12 25   8 15 16 5

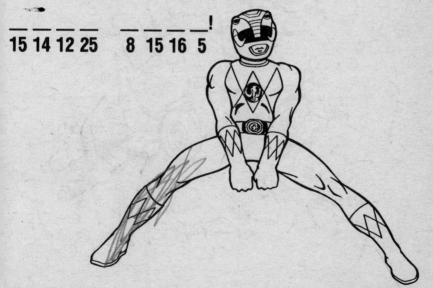

SEE ANSWERS.

21.
Connect the dots to draw a fierce-fighting Dinozord.

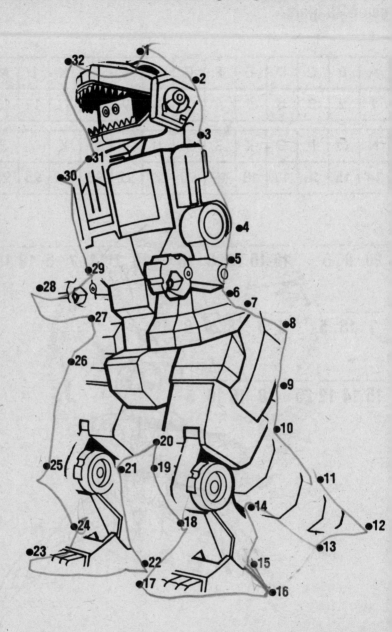

SEE ANSWERS

Unscramble the letters to identify the Power Ranger who uses this coin.

L E U B

_ _ _ _

N A G R E R

_ _ _ _ _ _

SEE ANSWERS.

23.
**Follow the path that leads through the Power Coins to
the Power Morpher.**

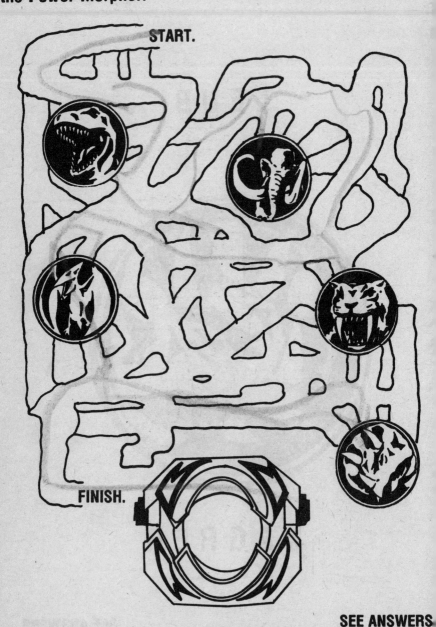

START.

FINISH.

SEE ANSWERS.

4.

Drop a letter in column A to spell a new word in column B. (You can rearrange the letters to spell the new word.) Then write the dropped letter in the circle to spell the mystery word.

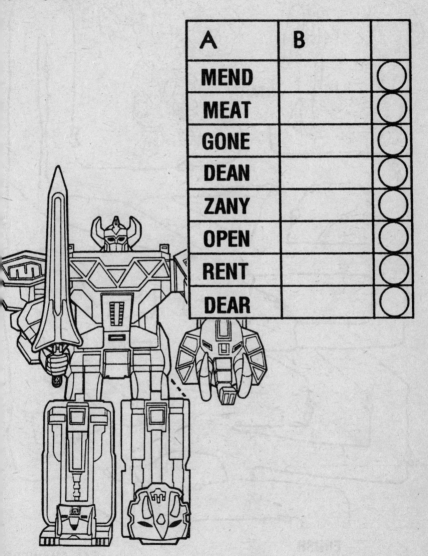

A	B	
MEND		◯
MEAT		◯
GONE		◯
DEAN		◯
ZANY		◯
OPEN		◯
RENT		◯
DEAR		◯

SEE ANSWERS.

25.
Jason and Zack must leap ahead of Goldar to "morph" into Power Rangers. Which path should they take?

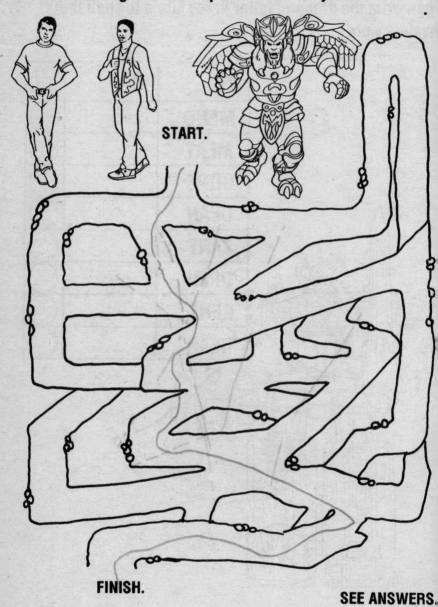

START.

FINISH.

SEE ANSWERS.

Unscramble the letters to find out which Power Ranger uses this Power Coin to "morph."

OWLYEL

_ _ _ _ _ _

NRGARE

_ _ _ _ _ _

SEE ANSWERS.

27.

Which teen turns into which Power Ranger? Match each teen to the right Power Ranger.

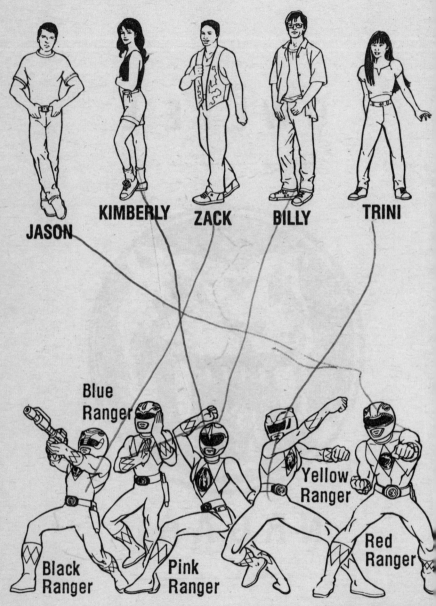

JASON KIMBERLY ZACK BILLY TRINI

Blue Ranger

Black Ranger Pink Ranger Yellow Ranger Red Ranger

SEE ANSWERS

8.

ow many times can you find Squatt in the picture?
ount carefully, many overlap.

SEE ANSWERS.

29.
Pick the path that leads Pterodactyl Dinozord to Kimberly, the Pink Ranger.

START.

FINISH.

SEE ANSWER

0.

Drop a letter in column A to spell a new word in column B. (You can rearrange the letters to spell the new word.) Then write the dropped letter in the circle to spell the mystery name.

A	B	
PANT		○
ODOR		○
WENT		○
TEEN		○
REAR		○
HARD		○
TALE		○
NICE		○
GONE		○
FIRE		○
RAIL		○
SOAR		○

SEE ANSWERS.

31.
Follow the path that turns the teens into Power Rangers.

START.

FINISH.

SEE ANSWER

32.
Connect the dots to draw Rita's wand.

SEE ANSWERS.

33.
Unscramble the letters to discover which Power Ranger uses this Power Coin.

IPKN

_ _ _ _

ARGREN

_ _ _ _ _ _

SEE ANSWERS.

4.

**ill in the missing letters to hear the Power Rangers'
ommand to create Megazord.**

D _ N _ Z _ R D S,
P _ _ _ R !

SEE ANSWERS.

35.
Draw your own Mastodon Dinozord.

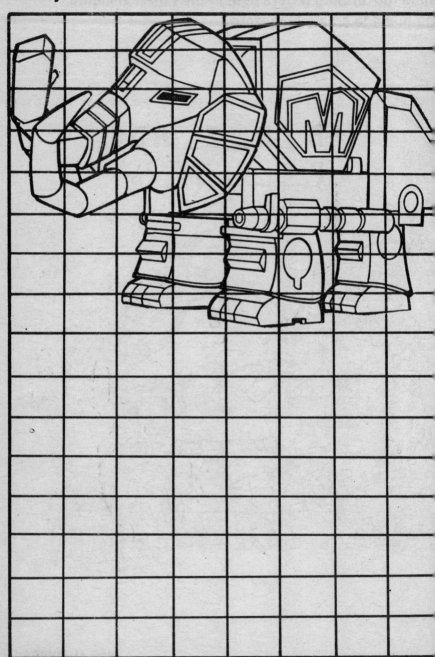

SEE ANSWERS

atch the Dinozord to the Power Ranger who calls it.

A.

B.

C.

D.

E.

1.

2.

3.

4.

5.

SEE ANSWERS.

37.

How many Mighty Morphin Power Rangers' bolts are in the picture? Count carefully, many overlap.

SEE ANSWERS

ick the path that leads Titanus to Megazord.

START.

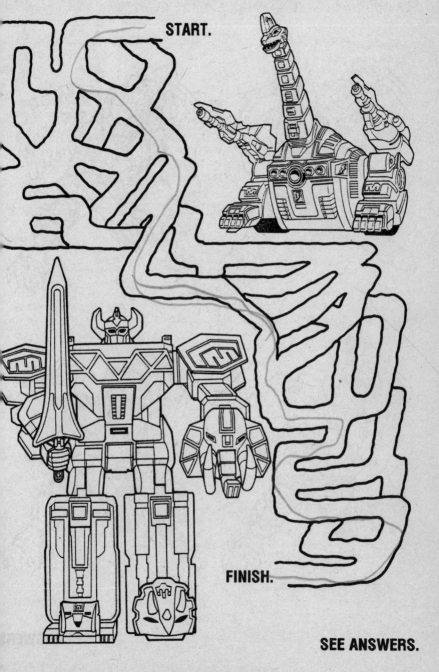

FINISH.

SEE ANSWERS.

39.
Which picture of Goldar is different from the others?

SEE ANSWERS

elp the Black Ranger find his way through the
lastodon Dinozord maze.

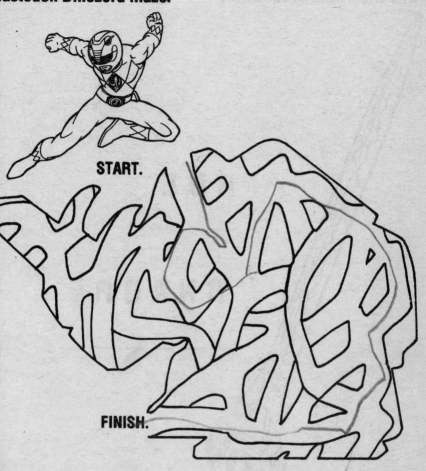

START.

FINISH.

SEE ANSWERS.

41.
Unscramble the letters that name a Power Ranger who wields the Silver Sword.

R D E
— — —

R N A G E R
— — — — — —

SEE ANSWERS

42.

Drop a letter in column A to spell a new word in column B. (You can rearrange the letters to spell the new word.) Then write the dropped letter in the circle to spell the mystery word.

A	B	
BROOM		◯
TAME		◯
TORE		◯
TART		◯
PILE		◯
PALE		◯
BAND		◯
PAID		◯
PLANK		◯
RODE		◯
LIST		◯

SEE ANSWERS.

43.

Which path leads Billy, the Blue Ranger, through the Triceratops Dinozord maze?

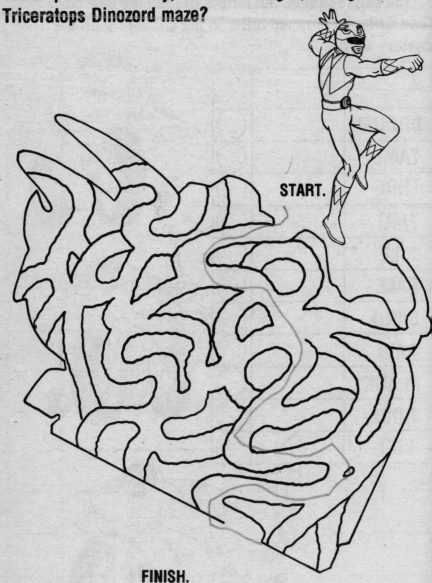

START.

FINISH.

SEE ANSWERS

44.

Draw your own Tyrannosaurus Dinozord.

SEE ANSWERS.

45.
Connect the dots to draw the Red Ranger's Battle Bike.

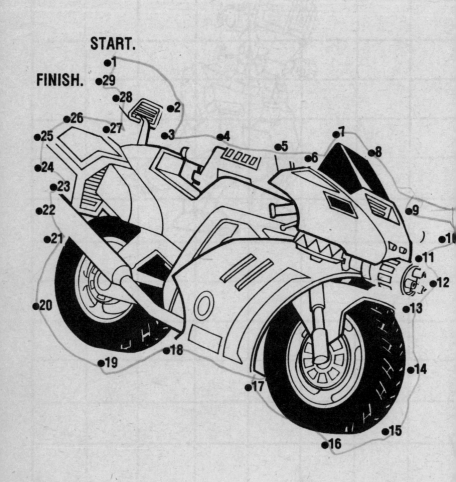

START.
FINISH.

SEE ANSWERS.

oldar is getting away. Pick a path that enables
egazord to catch this villain.

START.

FINISH.

SEE ANSWERS.

47.

Find the words and names listed below in the letter grid.
Look, up, down, forward, backward and diagonally.

ZORDON
MORPHER
KIMBERLY
COINS
ZACK
TRINI
BRAVE
JASON
ZORD
ALPHA 5
BILLY

```
B R A V E K C A Z S X E D
C Z E G I N I R T Y H N Y
L A O H M B V S D S D L J
U C I R P W E R N U R O A
M N B H D R V I U E O H S
Q Z I D E O O M B N Z R O
K L L M V C N M J D S K N
A S L D F G I H Z X C V B
N M Y Q W K E A L P H A 5
```

SEE ANSWERS

48.
Which two Red Rangers are exactly alike?

SEE ANSWERS

49.
Find the Putty Patrol hidden in the picture.

SEE ANSWERS

50.

Color in the spaces with a 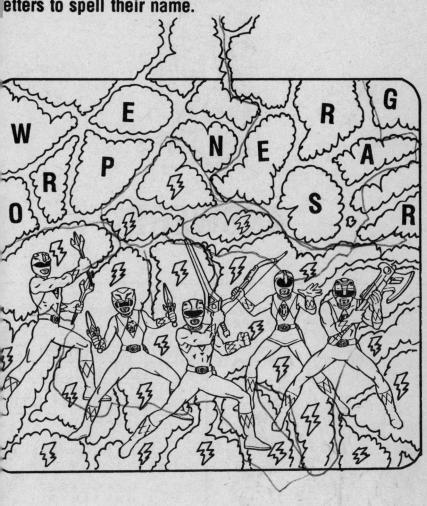 to find out who can win against Rita Repulsa. Then unscramble the remaining letters to spell their name.

_ _ _ _ _   _ _ _ _ _ _ _

SEE ANSWERS.

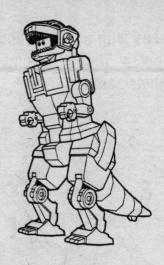

ANSWERS

1.
Who are the Mighty Morphin Power Rangers? To find out, follow the correct letter path to spell a message that describes them.

2.
Use the chart below to decode a message from the Power Rangers.

A	B	C	D	E	F	G	H	I	J	K	L	
1	2	3	4	5	6	7	8	9	10	11	12	

N	O	P	Q	R	S	T	U	V	W	X	Y	
14	15	16	17	18	19	20	21	22	23	24	25	

R I T A   R E P U L S A   I S   A N
18 9 20 1   18 5 16 21 12 19 1   9 19   1 1

E V I L   S O R C E R E S S.
5 22 9 12   19 15 18 3 5 18 5 19 19

low the path from Zordon to the teens so that he can
e them the Power Morphers.

START.

FINISH.

4.
Cross out the letters with a ⚡. Then write the
remaining letters in the order in which they appear to
read the message.

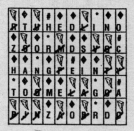

THE DINOZORDS
CHANGE INTO
MEGAZORD!

5.
low the path that takes the Yellow Ranger from one
of the Sabertooth Tiger Dinozord to the other.

START.

FINISH.

6.
Follow the correct path to spell the name of the Power
Ranger who drives the Mastodon Dinozord.

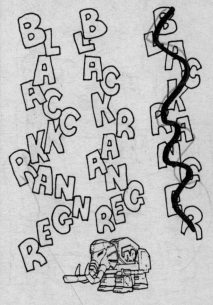

7.

Cross out every letter that appears 5 times. Then write the remaining letters backwards to read the message.

X	D	M	R	Y	X
O	M	Z	R	B	R	E	I
R	X	X	R	A	C	M	E
H	T	R	S	I	S	X	U
N	R	B	M	X	X	A	X
X	R	R	T	X	M	I	T

I I T A N U S   I S   I H E
C A R R I E R   Z O R D.

8.

Fill in the missing vowels (AEIOU) to spell the names of the teens who become Power Rangers.

1. T R I N I
2. B I L L Y
3. Z A C K
4. K I M B E R L Y
5. J A S O N

9.

Help the Blue Ranger break free from the clutches of Baboo. Which path leads him to safety?

START.

FINISH.

10.

Unscramble the letters to spell the name of a Dinozord that resembles an elephant.

TAONODMS
MASTODON

1.
Draw your own King Sphinx.

12.
Rita Repulsa's Evil Space Aliens are a motley crew of criminals. Lead the Power Rangers to their hiding place.

START.

FINISH.

Drop a letter in column A to spell a new word in column B. (You can rearrange the letters to spell the new word.) Then write the dropped letter in the circle to spell the mystery word.

A	B	
ZEST	SET	(Z)
OPEN	PEN	(O)
RATE	ATE	(R)
CARD	CAR	(D)
MOAT	MAT	(O)
ANT	AT	(N)

14.
The Red Ranger has summoned the Tyrannosaurus Dinozord. Which path unites them?

START.

FINISH.

15.
Drop a letter in column A to spell a new word in column B. (You can rearrange the letters to spell the new word.) Then write the dropped letter in the circle to spell the mystery name.

A	B	
RAID	AID	(R)
TIME	MET	(I)
TAPE	APE	(T)
READ	RED	(A)
REEL	EEL	(R)
TAPE	TAP	(E)
PLACE	LACE	(P)
FEUD	FED	(U)
LAMP	AMP	(L)
SEAT	EAT	(S)
MEAN	MEN	(A)

16.
Alpha 5 leads the teens to the Command Center and to a meeting with Zordon. Which trail does he take?

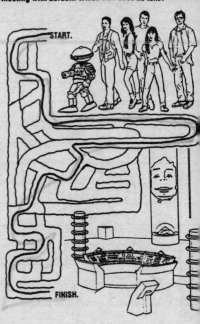

17.
Draw your own Power Morpher.

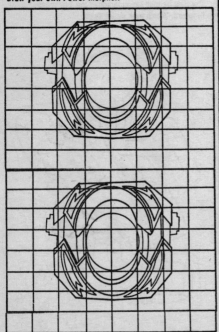

18.
The Putty Patrol retreats. Which path does it take to fle

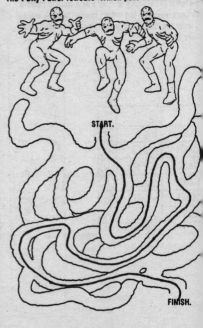

att must deliver a message to Rita Repulsa. Pick the
n that takes him to her headquarters.

RT.

FINISH.

20.
Use the chart below to decode a message from the
Power Rangers.

A	B	C	D	E	F	G	H	I	J	K	L	M
1	2	3	4	5	6	7	8	9	10	11	12	13

N	O	P	Q	R	S	T	U	V	W	X	Y	Z
14	15	16	17	18	19	20	21	22	23	24	25	26

THE   POWER   RANGERS
20 8 5   16 15 23 5 18   18 1 14 7 5 18 19

ARE   EARTH'S
1 18 5   5 1 18 20 8 19

ONLY   HOPE!
15 14 12 25   8 15 16 5

nnect the dots to draw a fierce-fighting Dinozord.

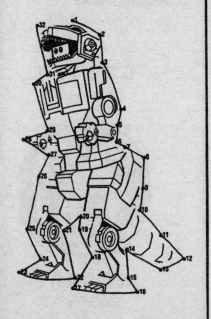

22.
Unscramble the letters to identify the Power Ranger who
uses this coin.

LEUB
BLUE

NAGRER
RANGER

23.

Follow the path that leads through the Power Coins to the Power Morpher.

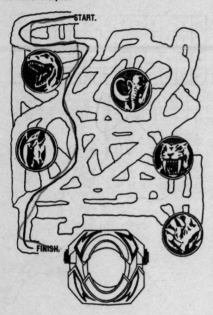

START.

FINISH.

24.

Drop a letter in column A to spell a new word in column B. (You can rearrange the letters to spell the new word.) Then write the dropped letter in the circle to spell the mystery word.

A	B	
MEND	END	M
MEAT	MAT	E
GONE	ONE	G
DEAN	DEN	A
ZANY	ANY	Z
OPEN	PEN	O
RENT	NET	R
DEAR	EAR	D

25.

Jason and Zack must leap ahead of Goldar to "morph" into Power Rangers. Which path should they take?

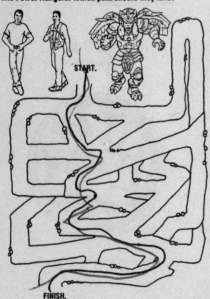

START.

FINISH.

26.

Unscramble the letters to find out which Power Ranger uses this Power Coin to "morph."

O W L Y E L
Y E L L O W

N R G A R E
R A N G E R

7.

Which teen turns into which Power Ranger? Match each teen to the right Power Ranger.

JASON   KIMBERLY   ZACK   BILLY   TRINI

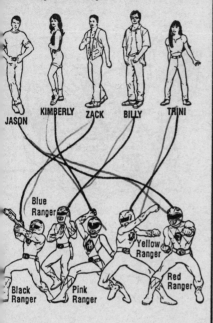

Blue Ranger

Yellow Ranger

Red Ranger

Black Ranger   Pink Ranger

28.

How many times can you find Squatt in the picture? Count carefully, many overlap.

Track the path that leads Pterodactyl Dinozord to Kimberly, the Pink Ranger.

START.

FINISH.

30.

Drop a letter in column A to spell a new word in column B. (You can rearrange the letters to spell the new word.) Then write the dropped letter in the circle to spell the mystery name.

A	B	
PANT	ANT	P
ODOR	ROD	O
WENT	NET	W
TEEN	TEN	E
REAR	EAR	R
HARD	HAD	R
TALE	LET	A
NICE	ICE	N
GONE	ONE	G
FIRE	FIR	E
RAIL	AIL	R
SOAR	OAR	S

31.
Follow the path that turns the teens into Power Rangers.

START.

FINISH.

32.
Connect the dots to draw Rita's wand.

33.
Unscramble the letters to discover which Power Ranger uses this Power Coin.

IPKN

P I N K

ARGREN

R A N G E R

34.
Fill in the missing letters to hear the Power Rangers' command to create Megazord.

D I N O Z O R D S,
" P O W E R "!

35.
Draw your own Mastodon Dinozord.

36.
Match the Dinozord to the Power Ranger who calls it.

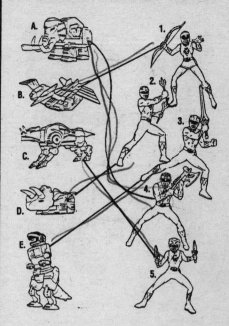

37.
How many Mighty Morphin Power Rangers' bolts are in the picture? Count carefully, many overlap.

38.
Pick the path that leads Titanus to Megazord.

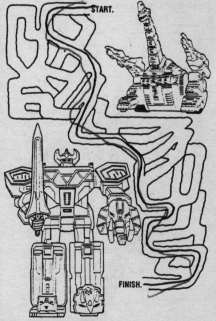

39.
Which picture of Goldar is different from the others?

40.
Help the Black Ranger find his way through the Mastodon Dinozord maze.

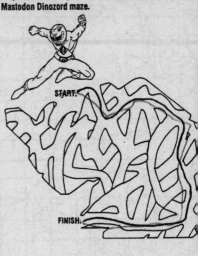

START.

FINISH.

41.
Unscramble the letters that name a Power Ranger who wields the Silver Sword.

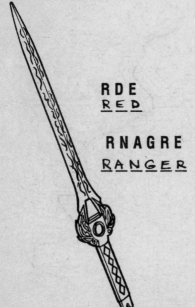

RDE
<u>RED</u>

RNAGRE
<u>RANGER</u>

42.
Drop a letter in column A to spell a new word in column B. (You can rearrange the letters to spell the new word.) Then write the dropped letter in the circle to spell the mystery word.

A	B	
BROOM	ROOM	(B)
TAME	MET	(A)
TORE	ORE	(T)
TART	ART	(T)
PILE	PIE	(L)
PALE	PAL	(E)
BAND	AND	(B)
PAID	PAD	(I)
PLANK	PLAN	(K)
RODE	ROD	(E)
LIST	LIT	(S)

ch path leads Billy, the Blue Ranger, through the eratops Dinozord maze?

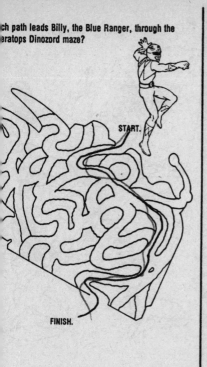

START.

FINISH.

44.
Draw your own Tyrannosaurus Dinozord.

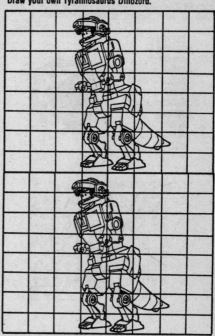

ect the dots to draw the Red Ranger's Battle Bike.

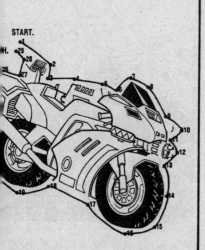

START.

46.
Goldar is getting away. Pick a path that enables Megazord to catch this villain.

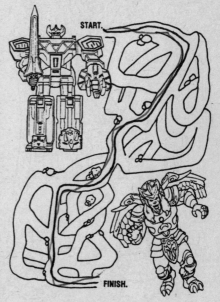

START.

FINISH.

47.
Find the words and names listed below in the letter grid.
Look, up, down, forward, backward and diagonally.

ZORDON
MORPHER
KIMBERLY
COINS
ZACK
TRINI
BRAVE
JASON
ZORD
ALPHA 5
BILLY

48.
Which two Red Rangers are exactly alike?

49.
Find the Putty Patrol hidden in the picture.

50.
Color in the spaces with a ✓ to find out who can w
against Rita Repulsa. Then unscramble the remainin
letters to spell their name.

POWER RANGERS